THIS JOURNAL BELONGS TO:

-

Made in the USA
Las Vegas, NV
12 December 2024

13963559R00073